John Russell Amberley

The Case of the Jews in the Matter of the Founder of

Christianity

John Russell Amberley

The Case of the Jews in the Matter of the Founder of Christianity

ISBN/EAN: 9783337026912

Printed in Europe, USA, Canada, Australia, Japan

Cover: Foto ©Lupo / pixelio.de

More available books at **www.hansebooks.com**

THE CASE OF THE JEWS

IN THE MATTER OF THE

FOUNDER OF CHRISTIANITY,

AS CONCEIVED BY

VISCOUNT AMBERLEY.

EXTRACTED FROM HIS WORK, "AN ANALYSIS OF
RELIGIOUS BELIEF."

WITH

INTRODUCTORY PREFACE

BY

H. GUEDALLA, ESQ.

LONDON.

1887.

PREFACE.

No Jewish author before Graetz has delineated the life of Jesus as he conceived it from the point of view afforded by his religion. It is owing to this enforced silence, for fear of punishment for blasphemy, that so much rancour has existed against them for nearly nineteen centuries.

The late Viscount Amberley, in his remarkable work, entitled "An Analysis of Religious Belief," has presented their case in a light which, from youth, has always occurred to me, and no doubt to many others in thought. The conclusions arrived at are : that as regards the crucifixion the spiritual rulers of Judæa were not so much to blame as has been commonly supposed, and were undoubtedly right judged by the principles of their own religion.

It occupies from page 379 to 421 of Volume 1st of Lord Amberley's book. It is an excellent defence, and uttered by him in a belief of its truth. "The more knowledge the more charity;" and however much I may dissent from the other portions of his book, I cannot but regret his premature death, and at the same time admire his bold advocacy from conviction in beliefs opposed to the orthodox tenets of Christianity. I do not think any Jew could have at any period more ably argued their side of the controversy. I am sure its perusal by Christians, actuated by brotherly love and kindness, will tend still further to cement union of interests with us, and its perusal by Jews cause them to admire the loving depth of Lord Amberley's heart, his fervent spirit, and the solemn purpose of the book, sparkling, as it does, with goodness, nobleness, and love. I, therefore, extract the chapter *in extenso*, being vastly superior to my early essay on the same subject penned forty years ago.

From an impartial view also of the question, the Jews ought actually to have been considered merely as the agents of Providence for the accomplishment of a certain end, and not therefore to be punished unrelentingly for ages under a false belief that the perpetrators where inflicting Divine vengeance by their terrible and cruel oppression.

H. GUEDALLA.

December, 1886.

VISCOUNT AMBERLEY'S

VINDICATION OF THE JEWS.

VICTORIOUS over Jesus Christ at the moment, the Jewish nation have, from an early period in Christian history, been subject in their turn to his disciples. Their polity—crushed under the iron heel of Vespasian, scattered to the winds by Hadrian—vanished from existence not long after it had successfully put down the founder of the new faith. Their religion, tolerated by the heathen Romans only under humiliating and galling conditions, persecuted almost to death by the Christians, suffered until modern times an oppression so terrible and so cruel, that but for the deep and unshakeable attachment of its adherents, it could never have survived its perils. Hence the course of events has been such that this unhappy nation has never until quite recently enjoyed the freedom necessary to present their case in the matter of Jesus the son of Joseph ; while the gradual decay of the rancour formerly felt against them, at the same time that it gives them liberty, renders it less important for them to come forward in what would still be an unpopular cause. Thus it happens that one side only in the controversy, that of the Christians, has been adequately heard. They certainly have not shrunk from the presentation of their views. Every epithet that scorn, hatred, or indignation could suggest has been heaped upon the generation of Jews who were the immediate instigators of the execution of Jesus, while all the subsequent miseries of their race have been regarded—by the party which delighted to inflict them—as exhibitions of the divine vengeance against that one criminal act. Nor have even free-thinkers shrunk from condemning the Jews as guilty of gross and unpardonable persecution, and that towards one who, if they do not think him a God, nevertheless appears to them singularly free from blame. On the one side, according to the prevailing conception, stands the innocent victim ; on the other the bloodthirsty Jewish people. All good is with the one ; all evil with the other. It is supposed that only their hard-heartedness, their aversion to the pure doctrine of the Redeemer, their determination to shut their eyes to the light and their ears to the words of truth, could have led them to the commission of so great a crime.

Whether or not this theory be true, it at least suffers from the vice of having been adopted without due examination. An opinion can rest on no solid basis unless its opposite has been duly supported by competent defenders. Now in the present instance this has not happened. · Owing to the causes mentioned above, the Christian view has been practically uncontested, and writer after writer has taken it up and repeated it in the unreflecting way in which we all of us repeat assertions about which there is no dispute. Yet a very little consideration will show that so simple an explanation of the transaction has at least no *à priori* probability in its favour. That a whole nation should be completely in the wrong, and a few individuals only in the right, is a supposition which can be accepted only on the most convincing evidence. And in order even to justify our entertaining it for a moment, we must be in possession of a report of the circumstances of the case from the advocates of the nation, as well as from the advocates of the individuals who suffered by its action. A one-sided statement from the partisans of a convicted person can never be sufficient to enable us to pronounce a conclusive verdict against his judges. The most ordinary rules of fairness prohibit this. Yet this is what is commonly done. No account whatever of the trial of Jesus has reached us from the side of the prosecution. Josephus, who might have enlightened us, is silent. On the other hand, the side of the defence has furnished us with its own version of what passed, and from the imperfect materials thus supplied we must endeavour to discriminate between the two as best we can. To do this justly, we must bear in mind, that even though the charges produced against Jesus should not appear to justify the indignation of his accusers, it is at least unlikely that that indignation was altogether without reasonable cause. And painful as it may be to be compelled to think that Jesus was in the wrong, it would surely—had not long habit perverted our natural sentiments—be quite as painful to believe that a large multitude of men, impelled by mere malignity against a virtuous citizen, had conspired to put him to death on charges which were absolutely groundless. The honour of an heroic, and above all, of a deeply religious people, is here at stake. It is no light matter to deal in wholesale accusations of judicial murder against them. It would surely be a happier solution if it could be shown that the individual condemned was not absolutely guiltless. But possibly we may be able to elude either alternative. Just as, according to the able reasoning of Grote, the upright character of Sokrates may be compatible with a sense of justice on the part of the Athenians who condemned him to death, so it is conceivable that the innocence of Jesus may consist with the fact that the Jews who caused him to be crucified were not altogether without excuse.

An examination of this question must be conducted with a careful regard to the hereditary feelings of orthodox Hebrews in matters of religion ; with an attention to the conceptions they had formed of holiness, and consequently of blasphemy, its negation ; with a desire to do justice if possible to the very prejudices that clouded their vision, and to realise the intensity of the sentiment that ruled their national

life and bound them to uphold their law in all its
severe integrity. We must remember that the Jews
were above all things monotheists. Ever since, after
the captivity, they had put away every remnant of
idolatry, they had clung to the unity and majesty of
Jehovah with a stern tenacity which no alluring
temptations, no extremity of suffering had been able
to break. If they were now ready to persecute for
this faith, they had at least shown themselves able—
they soon showed themselves able again—to bear persecution for its sake. Their law, with its monotheis-
tic dogmas and its practical injunctions, was to them
supremely holy. Any attempt to infringe its precepts, or to question its authority, excited their
utmost horror. To set up any other object of
worship than that which it recognised, to teach any
other faith than that which rested on this foundation,
was blasphemy in their eyes. The happiness, nay,
the very existence, of the nation was bound up with
its strict observance. This may have been a delusion,
but it was one for which the existing generation was
not responsible. It had been handed down from
their ancestors, and had reached them with all the
sanctity of venerable age. If it were a delusion, it
was one which the compilers of the Pentateuch ;
which Josiah, with his reforming measures ; which
Ezra, with his purifying zeal ; which the prophets
and priests of olden times who had fought and
laboured for the religion of Jehovah, had mainly
fostered. They had succeeded but too well in im-

pressing upon the mind of the nation the profound conviction that, in order to ensure the favour of God, they must maintain every iota of the revealed truth they had received, and that his anger would surely follow if they suffered it to be in the smallest degree corrupted or treated with neglect.

Nevertheless the utmost efforts of the people to guard the purity of the faith had been rewarded hitherto with little but misery. Their exemption from troubles did not last long after the rebuilding of the temple. A prey now to the Seleucidæ, now to the Ptolemies, their native land the scene of incessant warfare, they enjoyed under the Asmonean kings but a brief period of independence and good government. Their polity received a rude shock from the capture of Jerusalem by Pompey; maintained but a shadow of freedom under the cruel tyranny of Herod; and fell at last—some time before the public appearance of Christ—under the direct administration of the unsympathetic Romans. A more intolerable fate could hardly be imagined. The Romans had no tenderness for their feelings, no commiseration for their scruples, no comprehension of their peculiar practices. Hence constant collision between the governers and the governed. It is needless to enter in detail upon the miserable struggles between those who were strong in material force and those who were strong in the force of conscience. Suffice it to say, that provocation on provocation was inflicted on the Jews, until at length the inevitable rebellion came, to be terminated by the not less inevitable suppression with its attendant cruelties. But in the time of Jesus the crisis had not yet come. All things were in a state of the utmost tension. It was of the highest importance to the people, and their authorities were well aware of it, that there should be nothing done that could excite the anger of their rulers. The Romans knew, of course, that no loyalty was felt towards them in Palestine. And the least indication of resistance was enough to provoke them to the severest measures. All that remained of independence to the Jews—the freedom to worship in their own way ; their national unity ; their possession of the temple ; their very lives—depended on their success in conciliating the favour of the procurator who happened to be set over them. The assertion by any one of rights that might appear to clash with those of Rome, even the foolish desire of the populace to honour some one who did not pretend to them, were fraught with the utmost danger. It was necessary for the rulers to prove that they did not countenance the least indication of a wish to set up a rival power.

Their task was the more difficult because the people were continually looking for some great national hero who should redeem them from their subjection. The conception of the " Messiah," the Anointed One, the King or High Priest who should restore, and much more than restore, the ancient glory of their nation, who should lead them to victory over their enemies and then reign over them in peace, was ineradicably imbedded in their minds. Consequently they were only too ready—especially in these days of overstrung nerves and feverish agitation under a hateful rule—to welcome any one who held out the chance of deliverance. The risk was not imaginary. Prophets and Messiahs, if they were not successful, could do nothing but harm. Theudas, a leader who did not even claim Messiahship, had involved his followers in destruction. Bar-cochab, who at a later time was received by many as the Messiah, brought upon his countrymen· not only enormous slaughter, but even the crowning misfortune of expulsion from Jerusalem. Now, although the high priests and elders no doubt shared the popular expectation of a Messiah, they were bound as prudent men to test the pretensions of those who put themselves forward in that character, and if they were imperilling the public peace, to put a stop to their careers. It was not for them, the appointed guides of the people, to be carried away by every breath of popular enthusiasm. They would have been wholly unworthy of their position had they permitted floating reports of miracles and marvels, or the applauding clamour of admirers, to impose upon their judgment. Calmly, and after examination of the facts, it was their duty to decide.

Jesus had professed to be the Messiah. So much, is indisputed. Could his title be admitted ? Now, in the first place, it was the central conception of the Messianic office that its holder should exercise temporal power. He was not expected to be a teacher of religious doctrines, for this was not what was required. The code of theological truth was, so far as the Jews were aware, completed. The Revelation they possessed never hinted, from beginning to end, that it was imperfect in any of its parts, or that it needed a supplementary Revelation to fill up the void which it contained. Whatever Christians, instructed by the gospel, may have thought in subsequent ages, the believers in the Hebrew Bible neither had ascertained, nor possibly could ascertain, that Jehovah intended to send his Son on earth to enlighten them on questions appertaining to their religious belief. This they thought had long been settled, and he who tried either to take anything from it or add anything to it was in their eyes an impious criminal. Such persons, they knew, had been sternly dealt with in the palmy days of the Hebrew state, and the example of their most honoured prophets and their most pious kings would justify the severest measures that could be taken against them. A spiritual reformer, then, was not what they needed : a temporal leader was. And this they had a perfect right to expect that the Messiah would be. The very word itself—the Anointed One, a word commonly applied to the king —indicates the possession of the powers of government.[1] Their prophecies all pointed to this conception

---

[1] The word מָשִׁיחַ, translated into Messiah, is of common occurrence in the Old Testament. It is occasionally used of the Hebrew people, with the intention of emphasising the fact of their being, as it were, a royal or privileged people, superior to all other nations. In nearly all

of the Messiah. Their popular traditions all confirmed it. Their political necessities all encouraged it. The very disciples themselves held it like the rest of their nation, for when they meet Jesus after his resurrection we find them inquiring, " Lord, wilt thou at this time restore the kingdom to Israel ? "[1] The conversation may be imaginary, but the state of mind which such a question indicates was doubtless real. The author represented them as speaking as he knew that they had felt. Now, if even they, who had enjoyed the intimate friendship of Jesus, could still look to him as one who would restore to Israel something of her bygone grandeur, was it to be expected that the less privileged Jews, who had inherited from their forefathers a fixed belief in this temporal restoration, should suddenly surrender it at the bidding of Jesus of Nazareth ? For he at least did not realise the prevailing notions of what the Messiah ought to be. For temporal sovereignty he was clearly unfit, nor does he seem to have ever demanded it. There

---

cases it is the king of Israel who is described as the Anointed ; David frequently bearing this title, and Kyros being, I believe, the only pagan monarch to whom it is given. This occurs in the well-known exhortation (Isaiah xlv. 1), " Thus saith the Lord to his Messiah Kyros," &c. The verb מָשַׁח, with which it is connected, signifies to anoint, with the special sense of conferring a peculiar holiness on the anointed object. Unction was applied to the kings, the high priests, the altar, the tabernacle, the sacred vessels, and other objects used in divine worship. It conveyed, therefore, a consecration both to things and persons, and with persons it was also the symbol of a divinely-given power.

[1] Acts i. 6.

was a danger no doubt that his enthusiastic followers might thrust it upon him, and that, thus urged, he might be tempted to accept it. But his general character precluded the supposition that he could ever be fit to stand at the head of a national movement. The absence, moreover, of all political enthusiasm from his teaching proved him not to be the Saviour for whom they were looking. His assertions that he was the Son of God, though they might provoke sedition and endanger the security of his countrymen, could bring them no corresponding good.

Christians have maintained that the Jews were entirely wrong in their conception of the Messiah's character, and that Jesus, by his admirable life, brought a higher and more excellent ideal than theirs into the world. They admire him for not laying claim to temporal dominion, and laud his humility, his meekness, his submissiveness, the patience with which he bore his sufferings, and the whole catalogue of similar virtues. It was, according to them, the mere blindness of the Jews that prevented them from recognising in him a far greater Messiah than they had erroneously expected. Moreover, they tell us that another of the mistakes made by this gross nation was the expectation of an earthly kingdom in which Christ was to reign, whereas it was only a spiritual kingdom which he came to institute. But who were to be judges of the character of the Messiah if not the Jews to whom he was to come ? The very thought of a Messiah was peculiarly their own. It had grown up in the course of their national history, and was embodied in their national prophecies. They alone were its authorised interpreters; they alone could say whether it was fulfilled in the case of a given individual. It is surely a piece of the most amazing presumption on the part of nations of heathen origin to pretend that they are more competent than the Jews themselves to understand the meaning of a Jewish term, a term, moreover, which neither had nor could have before the time of Jesus any sense at all except that which the Jews themselves attached to it. Christians, who derive not only their idea of the Messiah's character, but their very knowledge of the word, from the case of Jesus alone, undertake to set right the Jews, among whom it was a current notion for centuries before he had been conceived in his mother's womb!

Granting, however, that this difficulty might have been surmounted, supposing that it was a spiritual kingdom which the ancient prophets under uncouth images referred to, the question still remains whether Jesus in other respects fulfilled the conditions demanded by Scripture. For this purpose it will be the fairest method to confine ourselves to the discussion of those prophecies alone which are quoted by the Evangelists, and are therefore relied upon by them as proving their case. Where, however, they have quoted only a portion of a prophecy, and the remainder gives a somewhat different complexion to the passage extracted, justice to their opponents requires that we should consider the whole.

Take first the circumstances of Christ's birth. It was expected that the Messiah was to be of the family of David, and born at Bethlehem Ephrathah. Now, according to two of our authorities, he fulfilled both of these conditions. But, without at all discussing the point whether their statement is true, it is abundantly sufficient for the vindication of the Jews to observe, that they neither knew, nor could know, anything at all, either of his royal lineage or of his birth at Bethlehem. For he himself never stated either of the two capital facts of which Luke and Matthew make so much, nor does it appear that any of his disciples alluded to them during his lifetime. He was habitually spoken about as Jesus of Nazareth. Matthew, in endeavouring to account for the name by misquoting a prophecy, bears witness to the fact that it expressed the general belief. Luke makes him speak of Nazareth as his own country. Nowhere does it appear that he repudiated the implication conveyed by his ordinary title. Still less did he ever maintain—what his over-busy biographers maintained for him—that he was of the seed of David. Quite the reverse. He contends against the Pharisees that the Messiah was not to be a descendant of David at all. The dialogue as given by Matthew runs thus : "'What is your opinion about the Christ ? whose son is he ?' They say to him, 'David's.' He says to them, 'How then does David in the spirit call him lord, saying, The Lord said to my lord, Sit on my right hand until I place thine enemies under thy feet ? If then David calls him lord, how is he his son ? ' " [1] No answer was given by the Pharisees, nor was any explanation of the paradox ever granted them by Jesus. In the absence, then, of any further elucidation we can only put one interpretation upon his argument. It was clearly intended to show, not only that the Messiah *need* not, but that he *could* not be of the house of David. David in that case would not have called him Lord. The Pharisees may have been but little impressed by the force of the argument, but of one thing they could scarcely entertain a doubt. Jesus wished it to be thought that he was the Messiah. He also wished it to be thought that the Messiah was not a son of David. He himself therefore was certainly not a son of David. But if anything more were needed to excuse the ignorance— supposing it such—of the Jewish rulers about the birthplace and family of Jesus, we find it even super-abundantly in the work of one of his own adherents— the fourth evangelist. Not that this writer is to be taken as an authority on the facts, but he is an authority on the views that were current, at least in a portion of his own sect, and on that which he himself —writing long after the death of Christ—had received by tradition. Now, in the beginning of his Gospel he describes Philip the disciple as going to Nathanael,

---

[1] Mt. xxii. 2–45.

and saying, " We have found him of whom Moses in
the law and of whom the prophets wrote, Jesus *the
son of Joseph from Nazareth.*" At this Nathanael
sceptically asks, " Can anything good come from
Nazareth ? " and Philip replies, " Come and see."[1]
According to this account, then, the very disciples of
Jesus believed in his Nazarene nativity, as also (by
the way) in his generation by a human father. Nor
is this all the evidence. In another chapter an active
discussion is represented as going on among the Jews
as to whether Jesus was the Christ or not. Opinions
differed. Foremost among the arguments for the
negative, however, was the appeal to the Scriptural
declaration that the Christ must be of David's seed,
and emanate from the village of Bethlehem.[2] No
answer to this was forthcoming from the partisans of
Jesus, nor is any suggested by the Evangelist. There
is but one rational inference to be drawn from his
silence. He either had not heard, or he purposely
ignored, the story of Christ's birth at Bethlehem, and
the genealogies which connected him with David.
His mind (if he had ever been a Jew) was to no small
extent emancipated from Jewish limitations, and with
his highly refined views of the Logos, he did not
believe in the necessity of these material conditions.
It was nothing to him that they were not fulfilled.
More orthodox believers in the prophecies of the Old
Testament may be pardoned if they could not so lightly

---

[1] Jo. i. 45, 46.   [2] Jo. vii. 42.

put them aside. But what shall be said of the conduct of Jesus ? If he really were a descendant of David, born at Bethlehem, and wrongly taken for a Nazarene, can we acquit him of an inexcusable fraud upon the Jews in not bringing these facts under their notice ? Assuredly not. If, knowing as he did the weight they would have in the public mind, he kept them back ; knowing that they would overcome some of the gravest objections that were taken against his claim, he did not urge them in reply ; knowing at the close of his life that he was charged with an undue assumption of authority, he did not produce them as at least a portion of his credentials,—he played a part which it would be difficult to stigmatise as severely as it deserves. He believed that his reception by his nation would be an immense benefit to themselves, yet he did not speak the word which might have helped them to receive him. He thought he had a mission from God, yet he failed to use one potent argument in favour of the truth of that idea. He saw finally that he was condemned to death for supposed impiety, yet he suffered the Sanhedrim to incur the guilt of his condemnation without employing one of his strongest weapons in his defence. Happily, we are not obliged to suspect him of this iniquity. The contradictory stories by which his royal descent and his birth at Bethlehem are sought to be established sufficiently betray their origin to permit us to believe in the honour and honesty of Jesus.

Another Messianic prophecy which he is supposed

to have fulfilled is that of birth from a virgin, the necessity of which was deduced from an expression of Isaiah's. That the writer of the fourth Gospel was ignorant of this virgin-birth we have already shown, and that the Jewish people in general took him to be the son of Joseph is obvious enough from their allusions to his father.[1] Here again he never contradicted the prevalent assumption. But even had they known of the miraculous conception, the Jews might have denied that the passage from Isaiah bore any such construction as that put upon it by Matthew. He renders it: "Behold, the virgin shall be with child, and bear a son."[2] But a more proper translation would be: "The maiden shall conceive, and bear a son," for the word translated *virgin* by Matthew does not exclude young women who have lost their virginity. Nay, it curiously enough happens to be used elsewhere of maidens engaged in the very conduct by which they would certainly be deprived of it.[3]

---

[1] Mk. vi. 3 ; Mt. xiii. 55, 56 ; Lu. iv. 22 ; Jo. vi. 42.

[2] Mt. i. 23.

[3] The word עַלְמָה, improperly rendered παρθένος in the LXX., means, according to Fürst's Hebrew Lexicon, "a marriageable, ripe maiden, either unmarried, Gen. xxiv. 43 ; Ex. ii. 8 ; Song of Sol. vi. 8, . . . or in sexual intercourse with a man, Prov. xxx. 19."— Fürst, *sub voce.* The correct translation of this passage was given as early as the second century by Theodotion and Aquila, whom Irenæus refutes by the aid of a fabulous story to the effect that the seventy translators of the Old Testament each did his work separately, and that their seventy versions, when presented to Ptolemy, were found to be word for word the same. Thus, "even the Gentiles present perceived that the Scriptures had been interpreted by the inspiration of God."— Irenæus adv. Hær. iii. 21.

Moreover, the two prophecies quoted by Matthew, which were, no doubt, familiar to the Jews, could by no possibility be applied by them to a person of the character of Jesus. Even the small fragments torn away from their context by the Evangelist convict him of a misapplication. In the first fragment, the Virgin's son is called Immanuel, a name which Jesus never bore.[1] In the second, he is described as "a ruler, who shall govern my people Israel," which Jesus never was.[2] But the unlikeness of the predicted person to Jesus is still further shown by comparing the circumstances as conceived by the prophet with the actual circumstances of the time. Immanuel's birth is to be followed, while he is still too young to choose between good and evil, by a terrible desolation of the land. Hosts, described as flies and bees, are to come from Egypt and Assyria, and camp in the valleys, the clefts of the rocks, the hedges and meadows. Cultivable land will produce only thorns and thistles. Cultivated hills will be surrendered to cattle from fear of thorns and thistles.[3] Nothing of all this happened in the time of Jesus. But the prophecy of Micah is still more inappropriate. The "ruler" who is to be born in Bethlehem is to lead Israel to victory over all her enemies. He is to deliver his people from the Assyrian. The remnant of Jacob is to be among the heathen, like a lion among the beasts of the forest, like a young lion among flocks of sheep. Its hand is to be lifted up against its adversaries, and all its enemies are to be destroyed.[4]

---

[1] Mt. i. 23.   [2] Mt. ii. 6.   [3] Isa. vii. 14–25.   [4] Micah v.

These references to prophecy were certainly not happy. An allusion by Matthew to the words, " The people who walk in darkness see a great light," is not much more to the purpose, for Isaiah in the passage in question proceeds to describe the child who is to bring them this happiness as one who shall have the government upon his shoulder, who is to be on the throne of David, to establish and maintain it by right and justice for ever.[1] Another extract from Isaiah, beginning, " Behold my servant whom I have chosen," and depicting a gentler character, is more appropriate, but is too vague to be easily confined to any one individual.

Jesus himself is reported by one of his biographers to have relied on certain words from the pseudo-Isaiah as a confirmation of his mission. If the account be true, the circumstance is of great importance as showing the view he himself took of his office, and the means he employed to convince the Jews of his right to hold it. Entering the synagogue at Nazareth, he received the roll of the prophet Isaiah, and proceeded to read from the sixty-first chapter as follows :—" The Spirit of the Lord Jehovah is upon me, because Jehovah has anointed me to announce glad tidings to the poor ; he has sent me to bind up the broken-hearted ; to cry to the captives, Freedom, and to those in fetters, Deliverance ; to cry out a year of goodwill from Jehovah." Here Jesus broke off the reading in the middle of a verse, and declared that this day this scripture was fulfilled.[2] But let us con-

---

[1] Mt. iv. 15, 16 ; Is. ix. 1–7.　　　　[2] Lu. iv. 16–21.

tinue our study of the prophetic vision a little further. " To cry out a year of goodwill from Jehovah, and *a day of vengeance from our God ;* to comfort all that mourn ; to appoint for the mourners of Zion,—to give them ornament for ashes, the oil of joy for mourning, a garment of praise for a desponding spirit ; that they may be called oaks of righteousness, a plantation of Jehovah to glorify himself. And they will build up the ruins of old times, they will restore the desolations of former days ; and they will renew desolate cities, the ruins of generation upon generation. And strangers shall stand and feed your flocks, and the sons of foreigners shall be your husbandmen and your vinedressers. And you shall be called ' Priests of Jehovah ;' ' Servants of our God,' shall be said to you ; the riches of the Gentiles you shall eat, and into their splendour you shall enter."[1] Had Jesus concluded the passage he had begun, he could scarcely have said, " This day is this scripture fulfilled in your ears." The contrast between the prediction and the fact would have been rather too glaring.

Perhaps the most striking apparent similarity to Jesus is found in the man described in such beautiful language by an unknown prophet in the fifty-third chapter of Isaiah. But these words could hardly be applied to him by the Jews ; in the first place, because they would not be construed to refer to him until after his crucifixion, seeing that they describe oppression,

---

[1] Is. lxi. 1-6.

prison, judgment and execution ; in the second place, because there was no reason to believe that he bore their diseases, and took their sorrows upon him. And although the familiar words—doubly familiar from the glorious music of Handel,—" He was a man of sorrows, and acquainted with grief," may seem to us who know his end, to describe him perfectly, they could hardly describe him to the Jews, who saw him in his daily life. In that, at least, there was nothing peculiarly unhappy.

Failing the prophecies, which were plainly two-edged swords, Jesus could appeal to his remarkable miracles. He and his disciples evidently thought them demonstrations of a divine commission. But, in the first place, it is clear that the evidence of the most wonderful of these consisted only of the rumours circulating among ignorant peasants, which the more instructed portion of the nation very properly disregarded. Their demand for a sign[1] proves that they were not satisfied by these popular reports, if they had ever heard them. And in the second place, those miracles which were better attested were not convincing from the fact that others could perform them. Jesus, charged with casting out devils by Baäl-zebub, the prince of devils, adroitly retorted on the Pharisees by asking, if that were so, by whom their sons cast them out ?[2] But thus he admitted that he was not singular in his profession. Miracles, in short,

---

[1] Mt. xii. 38.   [2] Mk. iii. 22 ; Mt. xii. 24-30 ; Lu. xi. 14-24.

were not regarded by the Jews as any proof of Messiahship. Their own prophets had performed them. Their own disciples now performed them. Others might possibly perform them by diabolic agency. The Egyptian magicians had been very clever in their contest with Moses, though Moses had beaten them, and had performed far more amazing wonders than those of Jesus, in so far as these latter were known to the Pharisees.

Miracles being too common to confer any peculiar title to reverence on the thaumaturgist, there remained the doctrine and personal character of Jesus by which to judge him. It must be borne in mind that the impression which these might make upon his antagonists would depend mainly upon his bearing in his relations with them. He might preach pure morals in Galilee, or present a model of excellence to his own followers in Judæa ; but this would not entitle him to reception as the Messiah, nor would it remove an unfavourable bias created by his conduct towards those who had not embraced his principles. Let us see, then, what was likely to be the effect on the Pharisees, scribes, and others, of those elements in his opinions and his behaviour by which they were more immediately affected.

There existed among the Jews, as there still exists among ourselves, an institution which was greatly honoured among them, as it is still honoured, though in a minor degree among ourselves. The institution was that of a day of rest sacred to God once in every seven days. This custom they believed to have been founded by the very highest authority, and embodied by Moses in the ten commandments which he received on Sinai. Nothing in the eyes of an orthodox Jew could be holier than such an observance, enjoined by his God, founded by the greatest legislator of his race, consecrated by long tradition. Now the ordinary ·rules with regard to what was lawful and what unlawful on this day were totally disregarded by Jesus. Not only did his disciples make a path through a cornfield on the Sabbath, but Jesus openly cured diseases, that is, pursued his common occupation, on this most sacred festival.[1] When these violations of propriety (as they seemed to them) first came under the notice of the Pharisees, they merely remonstrated with Jesus, and endeavoured to induce him to restrain the impiety of his disciples. Not only did he decline to do so, but he expressly justified their course by the example of David, and by that of the priests, who, according to his mode of reasoning, profane the Sabbath in the temple by doing that to which by their office they were legally bound. Such an argument could scarcely convince the Pharisees, but they must have been shocked beyond measure when he proclaimed himself greater than the temple, and asserted his lordship even over the Sabbath-day. They then inquired of him—a perfectly legitimate question—

---

[1] Mk. ii. 23, iii. 7 ; Mt. xii. 1-14 ; Lu. vi. 1-11, xiii. 10-17, xiv. 1-6.

whether it was lawful to heal on the Sabbath, to which he replied that if one of their own sheep had fallen into the pit they would pick it out. Confirming his theory by his practice, he at once healed a man with a withered hand. It is noteworthy that the desire of the Pharisees to inflict punishment upon Jesus is dated by all three Evangelists from this incident; so that the hostility towards him may be certainly considered as largely due to his unsabbatarian principles.

Now in this question it is almost needless for me to say that my sympathies are entirely with Jesus. Although I do not perceive in his conduct any extensive design against the Sabbath altogether, yet it is much that he should have attempted to mitigate its rigour. For that the world owes him its thanks. But surely it cannot be difficult, in this highly sabbatarian country, to understand the horror of the Pharisees at his apparent levity. Seeing that it is not so very long since the supposed desecration of the Sunday in these islands subjected the offender to be treated as a common criminal; seeing that even now a total abstinence from labour on that day is in many occupations enforced by law; seeing that a custom almost as strong as law forbids indulgence in a vast number of ordinary amusements during its course, —we can scarcely be much surprised that the sabbatarians of Judæa were zealous to preserve the sanctity of their weekly rest. The fact that highly conscientious and honourable persons entertain similar sentiments about the Sunday is familiar to all. We know that any one who neglected the usual customs ; who, for example, played a game of cricket, or danced, or even pursued his commercial avocations on Sunday, would be visited by them with perfectly genuine reproaches. Yet this was exactly the sort of way in which Christ and his disciples shocked the Jews. To ·make a path through a cornfield and pluck the ears was just one of those little things which the current morality of the Sabbath condemned, much as ours condemns the opening of museums or theatrical entertainments. Their piety was scandalised at such a glaring contempt of the divine ordinances. Nor was the reasoning of Jesus likely to conciliate them. To ask whether it was lawful to do good or evil, to save life or to kill on the Sabbath-day was nothing to the purpose. The question was what *was* good or evil on that particular day, when things otherwise good were by all admitted to be evil. Nor were the cures effected by Jesus necessary to save life. All his patients might well have waited till evening, when the Sabbath was over. One of them, for instance, a woman who had suffered from a " spirit of weakness " eighteen years, being unable to hold herself erect, was surely not in such urgent need of attendance that a few hours more of her disease would have done her serious harm. Jesus, with his principles, was of course perfectly right to relieve her at once, but it is not to be wondered at that the ruler of the synagogue was indignant, and told the people that there were six working days ; in them therefore they should come and be healed, and not on the Sabbath. The epithet of " hypocrite," applied to him by Jesus, was, to say the least, hardly justified.[1]

Another habit of Jesus, in itself commendable, excited the displeasure of the stricter sects. It was that of eating with publicans and sinners. This practice, and the fact of his neglecting the fasts observed by the Pharisees, gave an impression of general laxity about his conduct, which, however unjust, was perfectly natural.[2] Here again I see no reason to attribute bad motives to his opponents, who merely felt as " church-going " people among ourselves would feel about one who stayed away from divine service, and as highly decorous people would feel about one who kept what they thought low company.

Eating with unwashed hands was another of the several evidences of his contempt for the prevalent proprieties of life which gave offence. The resentment felt by the Pharisees at this practice was the more excusable that Jesus justified it on the distinct ground that he had no respect for " the tradition of the elders," for which they entertained the utmost reverence. This tradition he unsparingly attacked, accusing them of frustrating the commandment of God in order to keep it.[3] Language like this was not

---

[1] Lu. xiii. 10-17.   [2] Mk. ii. 15-22 ; Mt. ix. 10-17 ; Lu. v. 29-39.
[3] Mk. vii. 1-13 ; Mt. xv. 1-9.

likely to pass without leaving a deep-seated wound, especially if it be true (as stated by Luke) that one of the occasions on which he employed it was when invited to dinner by a Pharisee. Indifferent as the washing of hands might be in itself, courtesy towards his host required him to abstain from needless outrage to his feelings. And when, in addition to the first offence, he proceeded to denounce his host and his host's friends as people who made the outside of the cup and the platter clean, but were inwardly full of ravening and wickedness, there is an apparent rudeness which even the truth of his statements could not have excused.[1]

Neither was the manner in which he answered the questions addressed to him, as to a teacher claiming to instruct the people, likely to remove the prejudice thus created. The Evangelists who report these questions generally relate that they were put with an evil intent : "tempting him," or some such expression being used. But whatever may have been the secret motives of the questioners, nothing could be more legitimate than to interrogate a man who put forward the enormous pretensions of Jesus, so long as the process was conducted fairly. And this, on the side of the Jews, it apparently was. There is nowhere perceptible in their inquiries a scheme to entrap him, or a desire to entangle him in difficulties by skilful examination. On the contrary,

---

[1] Lu. xi. 37-39.

the subjects on which he is questioned are precisely those on which, as the would-be master of the nation, he might most properly be expected to give clear answers. And the judgment formed of him by the public would naturally depend to a large extent on the mode in which he acquitted himself in this impromptu trial. Let us see, then, what was the impression he probably produced.

On one occasion the Pharisees came to him, "tempting him," to ascertain his opinion on divorce. Might a man put away his wife ? Jesus replied that he might not, and explained the permission of Moses to give a wife a bill of divorce as a mere concession to the hardness of their hearts. A divorced man or woman who married again was guilty of adultery. Even the disciples were staggered at this. If an unhappy man could never be released from his wife it would be better, they thought, not to marry at all.[1] Much more must the Pharisees have dissented from this novel doctrine. Rightly or wrongly, they reverenced the law of Moses, and they could not but profoundly disapprove this assumption of authority to set it aside and substitute for its precepts an unheard-of innovation.

Another question of considerable importance was that relating to the tribute. Some of the Pharisees, it seems, after praising him for his independence, begged him to give them his opinion on a dis-

[1] Mk. x. 1-12 ; Mt. xix. 1-12.

puted point : Was it lawful or not to pay tribute
to the Emperor ?   All three biographers are indignant
at the question. They attribute it as usual to a
desire to " catch him in his words," or, as another
Evangelist puts it, " to entangle him in his talk."
Jesus (they remark) perceived what one calls their
" wickedness," a second their " hypocrisy," and the
third their " craftiness."   " Why do you tempt me ? "
he began. " Bring me a denarium that I may see
it."   The coin being brought, he asked them,
" Whose image and superscription is this ? "
" Cæsar's."   " Then render to Cæsar the things
that are Cæsar's, and to God the things that
are God's." [1]   One of the Evangelists, reporting
this reply, rejoices at the discomfiture of the
Pharisees, who " could not take hold of his words
before the people."   Doubtless his decision had the
merit that it could not be taken hold of, but this
was only because it decided nothing.   Taking the
words in their simplest sense, they merely assert what
nobody would deny. No Pharisee would ever have
maintained that the things of Cæsar should be given
to God ; and no partisan of Rome would ever have
demanded that the things of God should be given to
Cæsar. But practically it is evident that Jesus meant
to do more than employ an unmeaning form of words.
He meant to assert that the tribute was one of the
things of Cæsar, and that because the coin in which

---

[1] Mk. xii. 13-17 ; Mt. xxii. 15-22 ; Lu. xx. 20-26.

it was paid was stamped with his image. More
fallacious reasoning could hardly be imagined, and it
is not surprising that the Pharisees "marvelled at
him." Nobody doubted that the Emperor possessed
the material power, and no more than this was proved
by the fact that coins bearing his effigy were current
in the country. The question was not whether he
actually ruled Judæa, but whether it was lawful to
acknowledge that rule by paying tribute. And what
light could it throw on this question to show that the
money used to pay it was issued from his mint ? It
must almost be supposed that Jesus fell into the confusion of supposing that the denarium with Cæsar's
image and superscription upon it was in some
peculiar sense Cæsar's property, whereas it belonged
as completely to the man who produced it at the
moment as did the clothes he wore. Had the Roman
domination come to an end at any moment, the coin
of the empire would have retained its intrinsic value,
but the Romans could by no possibility have founded
a right of exacting tribute upon the circumstance of
its circulation. Either, therefore, this celebrated declaration was a mere verbal juggle, or it rested on a
transparent fallacy.

After the Pharisees had been thus disposed of, their
inquiries were followed up by a puzzle devised by the
Sadducees in order to throw ridicule on the doctrine of
a future state. These sectaries put an imaginary case.
Moses had enjoined that if a man died leaving a
childless widow, his brother should marry her for the

purpose of keeping up the family. Suppose, said they, that the first of seven brothers marries, and dies without issue.' The second brother then marries her with the like result; then the third, and so on through all the seven. In the resurrection, whose wife will this woman be, for the seven have had her as their wife? To this Jesus replies : first, that his questioners greatly err, neither knowing the Scriptures nor the power of God ; secondly that when people rise from death they do not marry, but are like angels ; thirdly, that the resurrection is proved by the fact that God had spoken of himself as the God of Abraham, Isaac, and Jacob, and that he is not the God of the dead, but of the living.[1] Whether the Sadducees were or were not satisfied by this answer we are not told, but it is quite certain that their modern representatives could not accept it. For the inquirers had hit upon one of the real difficulties attending the doctrine of a future life. We are always assured that one of the great consolations of this doctrine is the hope it holds out of meeting again those whom we have loved on earth, and living with them in a kind of communion not wholly unlike that which we have enjoyed here. Earthly relationships, it is assumed, will be prolonged into that happier world. There the parent will find again the child whom he has lost, and the child will rejoin his parent ; there the bereaved husband will be restored

---

[1] Mk. xii. 18-27 ; Mt. xxii. 23-33 ; Lu. xx. 27-40.

to his wife, and the widow will be comforted by the sight of the companion of her wedded years. All this is simple enough. Complications inevitably arise, however, when we endeavour to pick up again in another life the tangled skein of our relations in this. Not only may the feelings with which we look forward to meeting former friends be widely different after many years' separation from what they were at their death ; but even in marriage there may be a preference for a first or a second husband or wife, which may render the thought of meeting the other positively unpleasant. And if the sentiments of the other should nevertheless be those of undiminished love, the question may well arise, Whose husband is he, or whose wife is she of the two ? Are all three to live together ? But then, along with the comfort of meeting one whom we love, we have the less agreeable prospect of meeting another whom we have ceased to love. Or will one of the two wives or two husbands be preferred and the other slighted ? If so, the last will suffer and not gain by the reunion. Take the present case. Assume that the wife loved only her first husband, but that all the seven were attached to her. Then we may well ask, whose wife will she be of them ? Will her affections be divided among the seven, or will they all be given to the first ? In the former case, she will be compelled to live in a society for which she has no desire ; in the latter, six of her seven husbands will be unable to enjoy the full benefit of her presence. The question is merely evaded by saying that in the resurrection there is neither marriage nor giving in marriage, but that men are like angels. Either there is no consolation in living again, or there must be some kind of repetition of former ties. Still less logical is the argument by which Jesus attempts to prove the reality of a future state against the Sadducees. In syllogistic form it may be thus stated :—

God is not the God of the dead, but of the living. God told Moses in the bush that he was the God of Abraham, Isaac, and Jacob. Therefore, they are not dead, but living.[1]

What is the evidence of the major premiss ? The moment it is questioned it is seen to be invalid. Nothing could be more natural than that Moses, or any other Hebrew, should speak of his God as the God of Abraham, Isaac, and Jacob, meaning that those great forefathers of his race had adored and been protected by the same Jehovah in their day, but not therefore that they were still living. The Sadducees must have been weak indeed if such an argument could weigh with them for a moment.

After this a scribe or lawyer drew from Jesus the important declaration that in his opinion the two greatest commandments were that we should love God with the whole heart, soul, mind, and strength ; and our neighbours as ourselves.[2] How gratuitous the imputations of ill-will thrown out against those who interrogate Jesus may be, is admirably shown in the

---

[1] Mk. xii. 18-27 ; Mt. xxii. 23-33 ; Lu. xx. 27-40.
[2] Mk. xii. 28-34 ; Mt. xxii. 34-40 ; Lu. x. 25-37.

present instance. One Gospel (the most trustworthy) asserts that the question about the first commandment was put by a scribe, who thought that Jesus had answered well, and who, moreover, expressed emphatic approval of the reply given to himself. Such (according to this account) was his sympathy with Jesus, that the latter declared that he was not far from the kingdom of God. Mark now the extraordinary colour given to this simple transaction in another Gospel. The Pharisees, we are told, saw that the Sadducees had been silenced, and therefore drew together. Apparently as a result of their consultation (though this is not stated), one of *them* who was a lawyer asked a question, *tempting him*, namely, which is the great commandment in the law ? Diverse again, from both versions is the narrative of a third. In the first place, all connection with the preceding questions is broken off, and without any preliminaries, a lawyer stands up, and, *tempting him*, inquires, " Master, by what conduct shall I inherit eternal life ? " To which Jesus replies by a counter-question, " What is written in the law ? " and then, strange to say, these two great commandments are enunciated, not by him, but by the unknown lawyer, whose answer receives the commendation of Jesus.

The bias thus evinced by the Evangelists, even in reporting the fairest questions, seems to show that Christ did not like his opinions to be elicited from him by this method, feeling, perhaps, that it was likely to expose his intellectual weaknesses. In this way, and possibly in others, a sentiment of hostility grew up between himself and the dominant sects, which, until the closing scenes of his career, was far more marked on his side than on theirs. Beautiful maxims about loving one's enemies and returning good for evil did not keep him from reproaching 'the Pharisees on many occasions. Unfortunately, a man's particular enemies are just those who scarcely ever appear to him worthy of love, and this was evidently the case with Jesus and the men upon whom he poured forth his denunciations. Judging by his mode of speaking, we should suppose that all religious people who did not agree with him were simply hypocrites. This is one of the mildest terms by which he can bring himself to mention the Pharisees or the scribes. Of the latter, he declares that they devour widows' houses, and for a pretence make long prayers ; therefore they would receive the greater damnation.[1] . The scribes and the Pharisees, it is said, bind heavy burdens on others, and refuse to touch them themselves (surely an improbable charge). They do all their works to be seen of men (their outward behaviour then was virtuous). One of their grievous sins is that they make their phylacteries broad, and enlarge the borders of their garments. Worse still : they like the best places at dinner-parties and in the synagogues (to which per-

---

[1] Mk. xii. 40 ; Mt. xxiii. 14.

haps their position entitled them). They have a
pleasure in hearing themselves called "Rabbi," a
crime of which Christ's disciples are especially to
beware. They shut up the kingdom of heaven,
neither entering themselves, nor allowing others to
enter. They compass sea and land to make one
proselyte, but all this seeming zeal for religion is
worthless ; when they have the proselyte, they make
him still more a child of hell than themselves. They
pay tithes regularly, but omit the weightier virtues ;
unhappily too common a failing with the votaries of
all religions. They make the outside of the cup and
platter clean, but within they are full of extortion
and excess. Like whited sepulchres, they look well
enough outside, but this aspect of righteousness is
a mere cloak for hypocrisy and wickedness. They
honour God with their lips, but their heart is far
from him.[1]

He uses towards them such designations as
these :—" Scribes and Pharisees, hypocrites ; " " you
blind guides ; " " you fools and blind ; " " thou
blind Pharisee ; " " you serpents, you generation
of vipers." If we may believe that he was the
author of a parable contained only in Luke, he used
a Pharisee as his typical hypocrite, and held up a
publican—one of a degraded class—as far superior

---

[1] Mt. xxiii. 1-33 ; Mk. vii. 6. I omit the concluding verses in Mt. xxiii.,
as the allusion in ver. 35 renders it impossible that Christ could have
uttered them. Indeed, the whole chapter is suspicious ; but as portions
of it are confirmed by Mark, I conclude that the sentiments at least, if
not the precise words are genuine.

in genuine virtue to this self-righteous representative of the hated order.[1]

Had the Pharisees been actually guilty of the exceeding wickedness which Jesus thought proper to ascribe to them, his career would surely have been cut short at a much earlier stage. As it was, they seem to have borne with considerable patience the extreme license which he permitted himself in his language against them. Nay, I venture to say that had he confined himself to language, however strong, he might have escaped the fate which actually befell him. And the evidence of this proposition is to be found in the extreme mildness with which his apostles were afterwards treated by the Sanhedrim, even when they acted in direct disobedience to its orders.[2] Only Stephen, who courted martyrdom by his language, was put to death, and that for the legal offence of blasphemy. Ordinary prudence would have saved Jesus. For his arrest was closely connected with his expulsion of the money-changers from the temple court. Not indeed that he was condemned to death on that account, but that this ill-considered deed was the immediate incentive of the legal proceedings, which subsequently ended, contrary perhaps to the expectation of his prosecutors, in his conviction by the Sanhedrim on a capital charge. Let us consider the evidence of this. For the convenience of persons going to pay tribute at the temple,

[1] Lu. xviii. 19-4.   [2] Acts iv. 15-21, and v. 27-42.

some money-changers, probably neither better nor
worse than others of their trade—sat outside for
the purpose of receiving the current Roman coin-
age and giving the national money, which alone
the authorities of the temple received in exchange.
Certain occasions in life requiring an offering of
doves, these too were sold in the precincts of the
temple, obviously to the advantage of the public.
Had Jesus disapproved of this practice, he might
have denounced it in public, and have endeavoured
to persuade the people to give it up. Instead of
this, he entered the temple expelled the buyers
and sellers (by what means we do not know), upset
the money-changers' tables, and the dove-sellers'
seats, and permitted no one to carry a vessel
through the temple. "Is it not written," he ex-
claimed, "'My house shall be called a house of
prayer for all nations?' but you have made it a den
of thieves." [1] The action and the words were alike
unjustifiable. The extreme care of the Jews to preserve the sanctity of their temple is well known
from secular history. Nothing that they had done
or were likely to do could prevent it from remain-
ing a house of prayer. And even if they had suffered it to be desecrated by commerce, was it, they
would ask, for Jesus to fall suddenly upon men
who were but pursuing a calling which custom
had sanctioned, and which they had no reason to

[1] Mk. xi. 15-18 ; Mt. xxi. 12-13 ; Lu. xix. 45-48.

think illegal or irreligious ? Was it for him to stigmatise them all indiscriminately as " thieves ?" Plainly not. He had, in their opinion, exceeded all bounds of decorum, to say nothing of law, in this deed of violence and of passion. Thus, there was nothing for it now but to restrain the further excesses he might be tempted to commit.

No immediate steps were, however, taken to punish this outrage. It is alleged that Jesus escaped because of the reputation he enjoyed among the people. At any rate, the course of the authorities was the mildest they could possibly adopt. They contented themselves with asking Jesus by what authority he did these things, a question which assuredly they had every right to put. He answered by another question, promising, if they answered it, he would answer theirs. Was John's baptism from heaven or from men ? Hereupon the Evangelists depict the perplexity which they imagine arose among the priests. If they said, from heaven, Jesus would proceed to ask why they had not received him ; if from men, they would encounter the popular impression that he was a prophet. All this, however, may be mere speculation ; we return within the region of the actual knowledge of the Evangelists when we come to their answer. " And they say in answer to Jesus, ' *We do not know.*' And Jesus says to them, ' *Neither do I tell you* by what authority I do these things.' " [1]

---

[1] Mk. xi. 27-33 ; Mt. xxi. 23-27 ; Lu. xx. 1-8.

Observe in this reply the conduct of Jesus. He had promised the priests that if they answered his question he also would answer theirs. They *did* answer his question as best they could, and he refused to answer theirs ! Even in the English version, where the contrast between him and them is disguised by the employment of the same word "tell" as the translation of two very different verbs in the original, the distinction between " We *cannot* tell" and "I *do not*," that is "will not tell," is palpable enough. But it is far more so in the original. The priests did not by any means decline to answer the question ; they simply said, what may very likely have been true, that they did not know whence the baptism of John was. In the divided state of public opinion about John, nothing could be more natural. They could not reply decidedly if their feelings were undecided. Their reply, "We do not know," was then a perfectly proper one. The corresponding reply on the part of Jesus would have been "I do not know by what authority I do these things ;" but this of course it was impossible to give. the chief priests, scribes, and elders had more right to ask Jesus to produce his authority for his assault than he had to interrogate them about their religious opinions. But Jesus, though he had for the moment evaded a difficulty, must have been well aware that he was not out of danger. It was probably in consequence of these events that he found it necessary to retire to a secret spot, known only to friends. Here, however, he was discovered by his opponents, and brought before the Sanhedrim to answer to the charges now alleged against his character and doctrine.

To some extent these charges are matter of conjecture. The Gospels intimate that there was much evidence against him which they have not ,reported. Now it is impossible for us to do complete justice to the tribunal which heard the case unless we know the nature and number of the offences of which the prisoner was accused. One of them, the promise to destroy the temple and rebuild it in three days, may have presented itself to their minds as an announcement of a serious purpose, especially after the recent violence done to the traders. However this may be, there was now sufficient evidence before the court to require the high priest to call upon Jesus for his reply. He might therefore have made his defence if he had thought proper. He declined to do so. Again the high priest addressed him, solemnly requiring him to say whether he was the Christ, the Son of God. Jesus admitted that such was his conviction, and declared that they would afterwards see him return in the clouds of heaven. Hereupon the high priest rent his clothes, and asked what further evidence could be needed. All had heard his blasphemy; what did they think of it ? All of them concurred in condemning him to death.[1]

---

[1] Mk. xv. 53-64 ; Mt. xxvi. 57-66 ; Lu. xxii. 66-71.

The three Evangelists who report the trial all agree that the blasphemy thus uttered was accepted at once as full and sufficient ground for the conviction of Jesus. Now, I see no reason whatever to doubt that the priests who were thus scandalised by his declaration were perfectly sincere in the horror they professed. All who have at all realised the extremely strong feelings of the Jews on the subject of Monotheism, will easily understand that anything which in the least impugned it would be regarded by them with the utmost aversion. And a man who claimed to be the Son of God certainly detracted somewhat from the sole and exclusive adoration which they considered to be due to Jehovah. As indeed the event has proved.; for the Christian Church soon departed from pure Monotheism, adopting the dogma of the Trinity; while Christ along with his Father, and even more than his Father, became an object of its worship. So that if the Jews considered it their supreme obligation to preserve the purity of their Jehovistic faith, as their Scriptures taught them to believe it was, they were right in putting down Jesus by forcible means. No doubt they were wrong in holding such an opinion. It was not, in fact, their duty to guard their faith by persecution. They would have been morally better had they understood the modern doctrine of religious liberty, unknown as it was to Christians themselves until some sixteen centuries after the death of Christ.

But for their mistaken notions on this head they were only in part responsible. They had inherited their creed with its profound intolerance. Their history, their legislators, their prophets, all conspired to uphold persecution for the maintenance of religious truth. They could not believe in their sacred books, and disbelieve the propriety of persecution. Before they could leave Jesus at large to teach his subversive doctrines, they must have ceased to be Jews ; and this it was impossible for them to do. We must not be too hard upon men whose only crime was that they believed in a false religion.

According to the dictates of that religion, Jesus ought to have been stoned. But the Roman supremacy precluded the Jews from giving effect to their own laws. Jesus was therefore taken before the procurator and accused of "many things." The charge of blasphemy of course would weigh nothing in the mind of a Roman ; and it is evident that another aspect of the indictment was brought prominently before Pilate ; namely, the pretension of Jesus to be king of the Jews. As to the substantial truth of this second charge, we are saved the necessity of discussion, for Jesus himself, when questioned by Pilate, at once admitted it. But whether it was made in malice, and in a somewhat different sense from that in which Pilate understood it, is not so clear. Jesus at no time, so far as we know, put forward any direct claim to immediate temporal dominion. At the same time it must be remembered that the ideas of Messiahship and possession of the kingdom were so intimately connected in the minds of the Jews, that they were probably unable to dissociate them. Unfit as Jesus plainly was for the exercise of the government, they might well believe that, if received by any considerable number of the people, it would be forced upon him as the logical result of his career. Nor were these fears unreasonable. His entry into Jerusalem riding on an ass (an animal expressly selected as emblematic of his royalty) with palm-branches strewed before him, and admirers calling "Hosanna" as he went, pointed to a very real and serious danger. Another such demonstration might with the utmost ease have passed into a disturbance of the peace, not to say a tumult, which the Romans would have quenched in blood unsparingly and indiscriminatingly shed. Jesus was really therefore a dangerous character, not so much to the Romans, as to the Jews. Not being prepared to accept him as their king in fact, they were almost compelled in self-preservation to denounce him as their would-be king to Pilate.

His execution followed. His supposed resurrection, and the renewed propagation of his faith, followed that. It has been widely believed that because Christianity was not put down by the death of its founder, because, indeed, it burst out again in renewed vigour, therefore the measures taken against him were a complete failure, and served only to confer additional glory and power on the religion he had taught. But this opinion arises from a confusion of ideas. If they aimed at preserving their own nation from what they deemed an impious heresy—and I see no proof that they aimed at anything else—the Jewish authorities were perfectly successful. Christianity, which, if our accounts be true, threatened to seduce large numbers of people from their allegiance to the orthodox creed, was practically extinguished among the Jews themselves by the death of Christ. They could not possibly believe in a crucified Messiah. Only a very small band of disciples persisted in adhering to Jesus, justifying their continued faith by asserting that he had risen from the tomb. But it was no longer among the countrymen of Jesus, whom he had especially sought to attach to his person and his doctrine, that this small remnant of his followers could find their converts. Neither then, nor at any subsequent time, has Christianity been able to wean the Jews from their ancient faith. The number of those who, from that time to this, have abandoned it in favour of the more recent religion has been singularly small. If, as is probable, there was during the earthly career of Jesus a growing danger that his teaching might lead to the formation of a sect to which many minds would be attracted, that danger was completely averted.

True, Christianity, when rejected by the Jews, made rapid progress among the Gentiles. But it was no business of the authorities at Jerusalem to look after the religion of heathen nations. They might have thought, had they foreseen the future of Christianity, that a creed which originated among themselves, and had in it a large admixture of Hebrew elements, was better than the worship of the pagan deities. Be this as it may, the particular form of error which the Gentiles might embrace was evidently no concern of theirs. But they had a duty, or thought they had one, towards their own people, who looked to them for guidance, and that was to preserve the religion that had been handed down from their forefathers uncorrupted and unmixed. This they endeavoured to do by stifling the new-born heresy of Jesus before it had become too powerful to be stifled. Their measures, having regard to the end they had in view, were undoubtedly politic, and even just.

For were they not perfectly right in supposing that faith in Christ was dangerous to faith in Moses ? The event has proved it beyond possibility of question Not indeed that they could perceive the extent of the peril, for neither Jesus nor any of his disciples had ventured then to throw off Judaism altogether. But they did perceive with a perfectly correct insight that the Christians were setting up a new authority alongside of the authorities which alone they recognised—the Scriptures and the traditional interpretation of the Scriptures. And it was precisely the adoption of a new authority which they desired to prevent. So completely was their foresight on this point justified, that not long after the death of Christ his assumed followers received converts without circumcision, that all-essential rite ; and that, after the lapse of no long period of time, Judaism was entirely abandoned, and a new religion, with new dogmas, new ritual, and new observances, was founded in its place. Surely the action of the men who sat in judgment upon Jesus needs no further justification, from their own point of view, than this one consideration. They had no more sacred trust, in their own eyes, than to prevent the admission of any other object of worship than the Lord Jehovah. Christ speedily became among Christians an object of worship. They owned no more solemn duty than to observe in all its parts the law delivered by their God to Moses. That law was almost instantly abandoned by the Christian Church. They knew of no more unpardonable crime than apostasy from their faith. That apostasy was soon committed by the Jewish Christians.

On all these grounds, then, I venture to maintain that the spiritual rulers of Judæa were not so blame-worthy as has been commonly supposed in the execution of Jesus of Nazareth. Judged by the principles of universal morality, they were undoubtedly wrong. Judged by the principles of their own religion, they were no less undoubtedly right.

DARLING AND SON,

MINERVA STEAM PRINTING OFFICE,

31, EASTCHEAP, E.C.

www.ingramcontent.com/pod-product-compliance
Lightning Source LLC
Chambersburg PA
CBHW022039080426
42733CB00007B/905